TO:

FROM:

Grandparents' Family Book

A KEEPSAKE
FOR OUR GRANDCHILD

Grandparents' Family Book

Charlie and Martha Shedd

ILLUSTRATIONS BY
MONA MARK

DOUBLEDAY & COMPANY, INC.
GARDEN CITY, NEW YORK
1982

Book design by Joe Caroff

Illustrations by Mona Mark

Library of Congress Catalog Card Number: 78-20098

ISBN: 0-385-13469-X

Copyright © 1982 by Charlie Shedd and Martha Shedd and The Abundance Foundation, Inc. Scriptural selections are from various versions of the Bible, including the authors' own translations.

All rights reserved

Printed in the United States of America

9 8 7 6 5 4 3 2

Contents

INTRODUCTION	*Charlie and Martha Shedd* 11
TO OUR GRANDCHILD 13	
HELPFUL HINTS 15	
PART I	*YOU* 17
PART II	*YOUR FATHER AND MOTHER* 37
PART III	*US—YOUR GRANDPARENTS* 51
PART IV	*THE FAMILY TREE* 65
PART V	*GENERAL FAMILY ATTITUDES* 77
PART VI	*THINGS WE DID TOGETHER* 83
PART VII	*MAJOR EVENTS OF YOUR WORLD AND SOME BEFORE THAT* 93
PART VIII	*SPECIAL DAYS, SPECIAL TIMES* 105
PART IX	*OTHER LITTLE THINGS WE THOUGHT YOU'D LIKE TO KNOW* 117
	SOMEDAY 127

Introduction

*"Tell ye your children of it,
and let your children tell their children,
and their children another generation."* **JOEL 1:3**

Introduction

"Tell me about when I was little; about when I was born; when I was in the play, the recital, the game, the hospital; about that funny thing I did in the Sunday-school program; what you thought when I made you the nail box; about the time I got lost in the woods."

All of us warm to stories about ourselves.

Why? Because we are put together with these nostalgic places in our hearts. And one thermostat that turns these very special warming places to their warmest glow is the fun remembering of our own history.

Then, we also like stories about our parents, brothers, sisters, cousins, aunts, uncles. But maybe the warmest glow of all comes from Grandpa and Grandma recall.

So wouldn't it be great if someone all the while was keeping a record? Then if that someone turned out to be an ultrasensitive friend like Grandpa or Grandma, wouldn't that be super?

At any age it would be fine, so very fine, to spend the evening with a personalized book on our family history. And wouldn't it be absolutely great to have a record bearing on the poet's theme "myself when young"?

This is who I am from baby days through childhood,
the shaping process, my youth, and all the happenings.

See all the fascinating facts about my pedigree, these tales
of my kinfolk, fine and not so fine.

Here are my ancestors, their record,
life-styles, what they did to earn their
bread, how they thought, their successes,
failures, beliefs.

It's all mine now,
mine for musing, because my grandparents cared that much.

Charlie and Martha Shedd

To Our Grandchild

Signed

Helpful Hints

Here are a few pieces of information that we feel should be of help to any grandparent.

Pedigree research can be a fascinating experience not only for you and your grandchild but for the entire family. For help in tracking the family roots, write to: Genealogical Research Associates, P.O. Box 11561, Salt Lake City, Utah 48147.

Practically every name that you could think of to bestow on your child or grandchild has a meaning and a history. There are several books to help you. You might start with *What to Name the Baby,* by Evelyn Wells, published by Doubleday & Company, Inc., Garden City, New York 11530.

Wouldn't it be fun to have the front page of a newspaper from the day your grandchild was born? Some large city papers can furnish these in certain issues. For an exciting addition to this book, contact the customer-service division of any major newspaper.

PART I

You

PART I

*"I am fearfully and wonderfully wrought,
and that my soul knoweth right well."* **PSALM 139:14**

You

"Lord, show me what I looked like when you first dreamed of me."

This is the prayer of a favorite friend. It is not by chance that he is a blessing to countless people. He says his favorite time for prayer is late of an evening.

When his family is in bed and the house is quiet, he sits in his big chair. Then, stilling himself, putting aside all other thought, he talks to the Lord. And in his visits with God, he always includes: "Lord, show me what I looked like when you first dreamed of me."

His report: "Not every night, but often enough, I actually get a glimpse of God's original intent for my life. I see me the way He first planned me, and I can tell you for sure, it's beautiful."

Blessed is the man who, in thoughts of his past, can honestly feel, "That was a good thing I did back there. I gave the man a break. I like to remember too some of the times I said 'no,' and other times I said 'yes' to a big challenge. Beautiful memories."

Blessed also is the woman who can muse, "The little thoughtful things I've done, I like to think about them: the phone call, letter, a meal I cooked for neighbors. Uncanny how often it was exactly the right thing at exactly the right moment. That was beautiful too."

Blessed are we all when we can honestly feel good about ourselves. A modern translation of Psalm 139:14 reads: "Isn't it amazing how we are put together? Sometimes I feel it in my heart."

Your grandparents would like to help you feel that way about yourself.

PART I

*"Tell ye your children of it,
and let your children tell their children,
and their children another generation."* **JOEL 1:3**

You

The day you were born

Date

Hour

Town

Hospital

Weight

Length

Coloring

Features

PART I

Your name

Why they chose your name

What your name means

PART I

First words

First doll

First bicycle

Other special toys

First pet

PART I

First words to a new brother or sister

First and/or most-significant illness or injury

First trip to the dentist

First haircut

PART I

First day of school

Name(s) of school(s)

Special events of school years

Favorite subjects

Your graduation day

PART I

Joining the Christian Community

Baptism

Minister

Church

Date   Time

Guests at Baptism

PART I

Communion

Confirmation

PART I

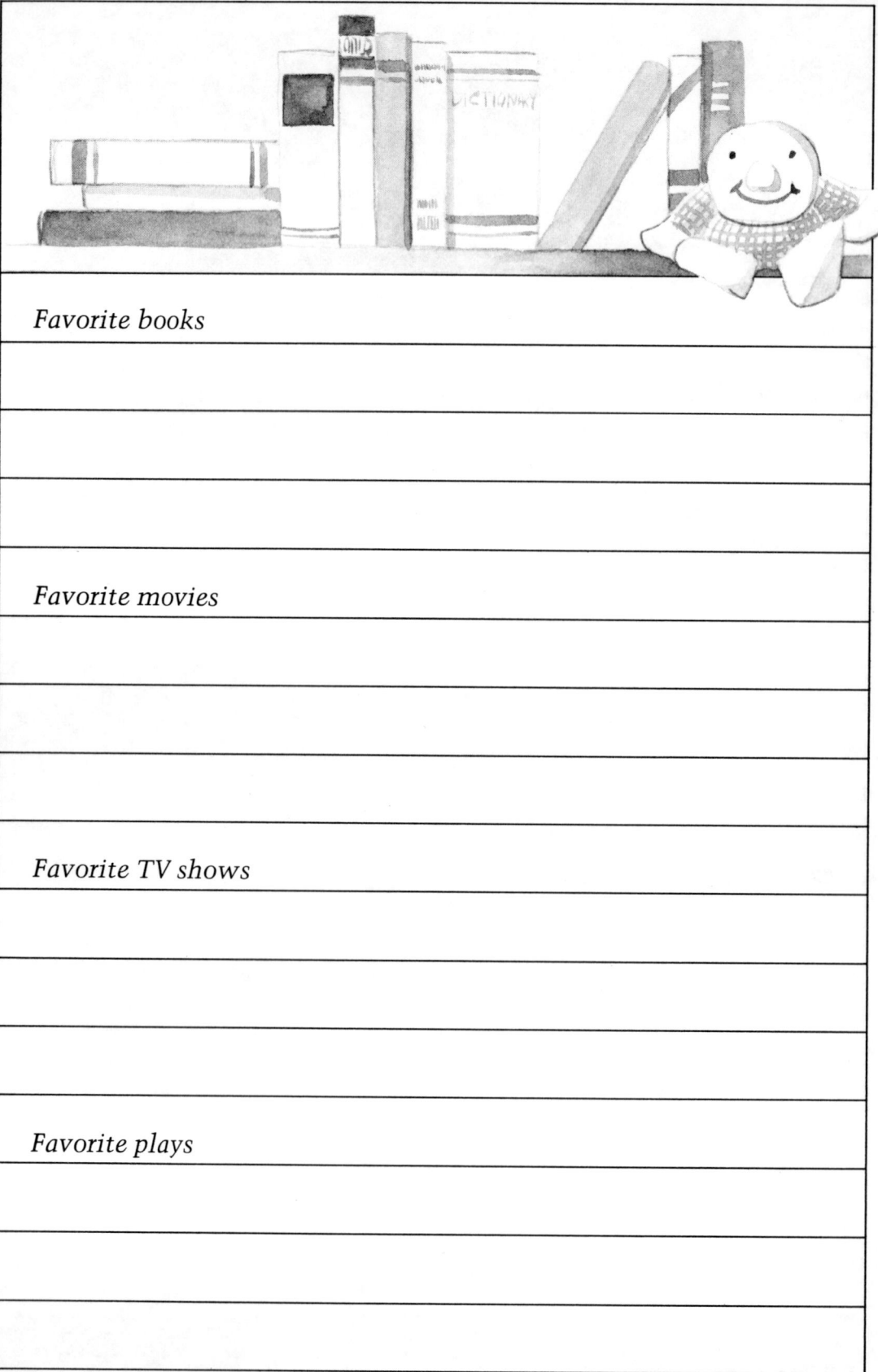

Favorite books

Favorite movies

Favorite TV shows

Favorite plays

PART I

High School Days

Name(s) of school(s)

Your graduation day

PART I

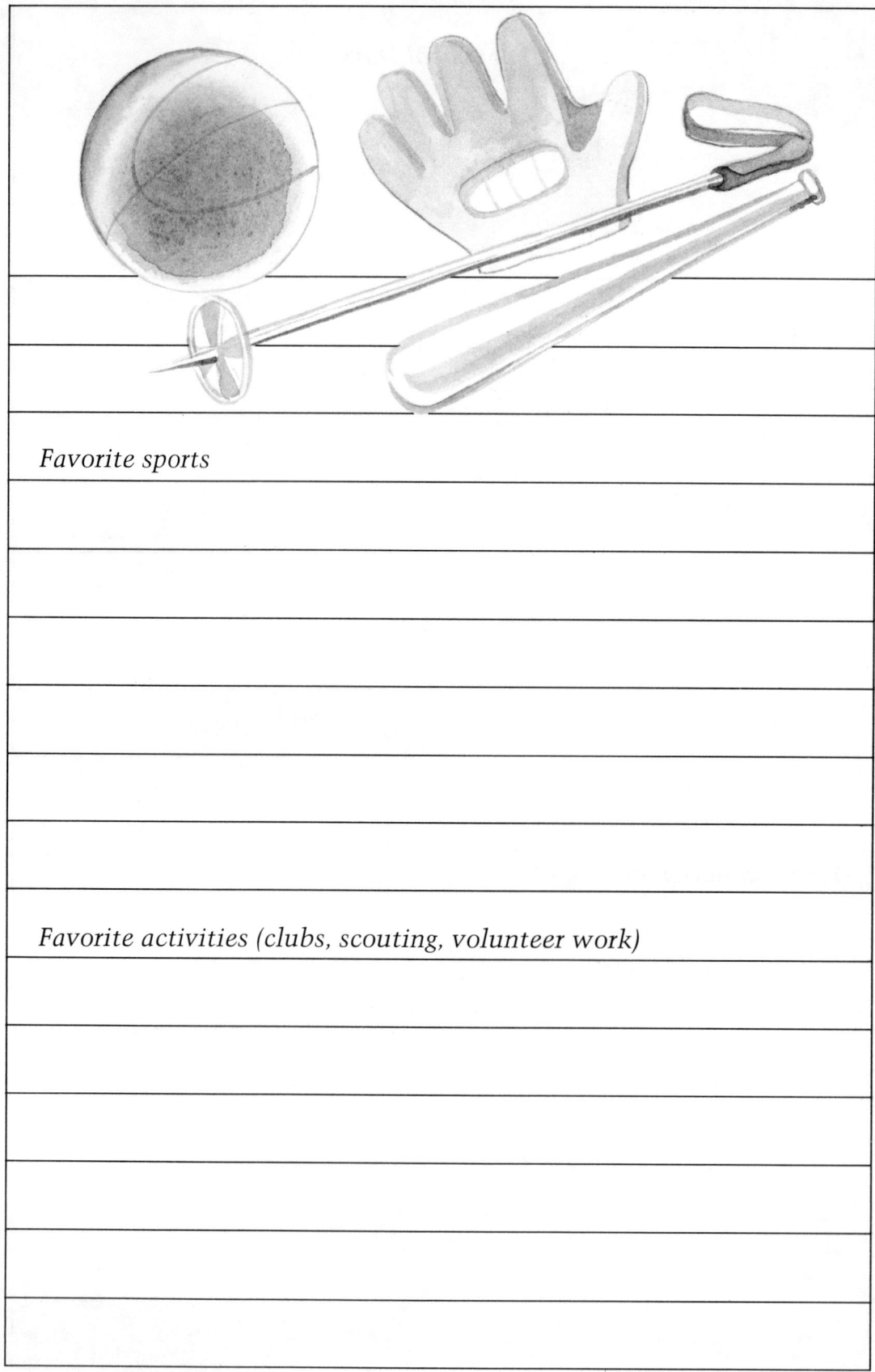

Favorite sports

Favorite activities (clubs, scouting, volunteer work)

PART I

Your special friends through the years

Favorite pets

Your favorite foods

Some of the places where you have lived: the town where you were born, first move, etc.

Military service

PART I

College Days

Name(s) of school(s)

Your graduation day

Graduate school(s)

PART I

*"Isn't it amazing how God put me together?
Sometimes I feel it in my heart."* **PSALM 139:14**

Other interesting items we remember and especially times we were proud of you (summer jobs, trips away from home, special honors and awards, athletic events, cooking, gardening, etc.)

PART I

Photographs

PART I

Photographs

PART II

Your Father and Mother

PART II

"Respect your father and mother."
EXODUS 20:12; DEUTERONOMY 5:16

Your Father and Mother

In a high school discussion group, the subject turned to "What I don't like about my parents." Nothing unusual there. It's a popular theme when the young get together. Except this gathering produced something different. Suddenly, in the midst of all that downbeat talk, the light came on in one boy. "Hey," he said (which for his age group is somewhat akin to "Now hear this"), "I just thought of something. If my parents are all that bad, how come I'm so wonderful?"

The commandment "Respect your father and mother" for most of us raises some questions. Were these

PART II

folks always utterly respectable? Probably not, and isn't that natural? In spite of our early-childhood awe, we know now that our parents were not perfect. Which means they couldn't have been altogether perfect in the way they handled us. Then, following that to its conclusion, we come out here: We must admit we probably weren't perfect either in our handling of their handling.

Solution! If we can accept all this philosophically and put their mistakes where they belong, then we can honor our parents where they were honorable, respect them where they performed respectably, and be grateful.
This has to be the fuller meaning of that all-important commandment:
"Respect your father and mother."

Your Father

Birth date
and place

Where he grew up

Went to school

Religious background

PART II

Accomplishments and special interests

Career employment history

Special service or military service

His brothers and sisters (nicknames)

PART II

Your Mother

Birth date and place

Where she grew up

Went to school

Religious background

PART II

Accomplishments and special interests

Career employment history

Special service or military service

Her brothers and sisters (nicknames)

PART II

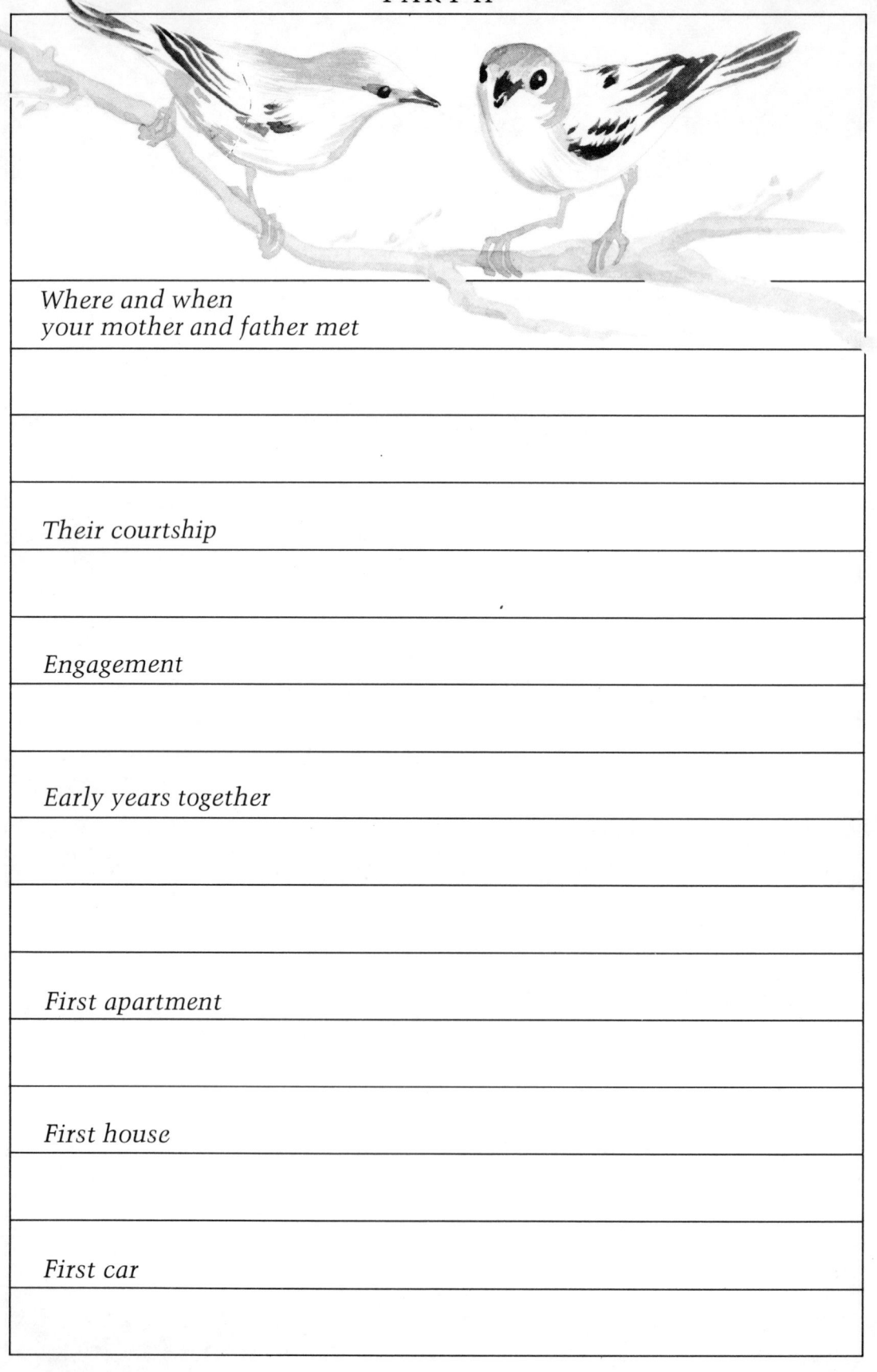

*Where and when
your mother and father met*

Their courtship

Engagement

Early years together

First apartment

First house

First car

PART II

Your Parents' Wedding

Place

Date *Time*

Maid (matron) of honor

Best man

Bridesmaids

Ushers

Reception place *Time*

Wedding trip

PART II

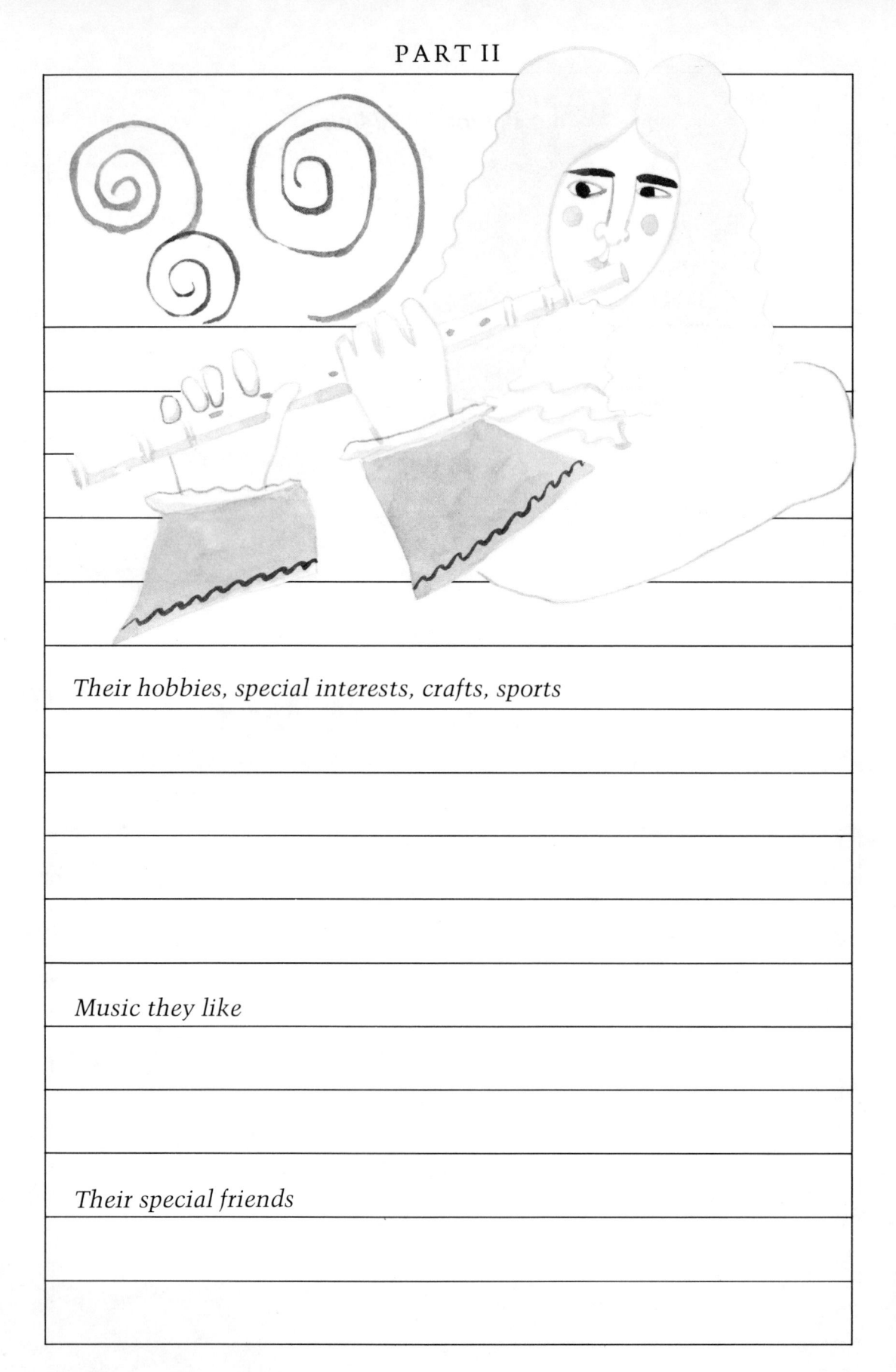

Their hobbies, special interests, crafts, sports

Music they like

Their special friends

PART II

Their church history and religious feelings

Their travels

Special events or situations they experienced (family achievements)

Places they lived

PART II

Photographs

PART II

Photographs

PART III

Us — Your Grandparents

PART III

*"I consider the faith that was
in thee and thy grandmother, Lois."* **2 TIMOTHY 1:5**

Us — Your Grandparents

Nostalgia is big these days. We love to remember, and we have reached a fine time in our development when the negative gives way to positive. It is a great day when bad times fade and the good begins coming on strong.

One source of happiness for all of us is memories from those who have been where we've never been. People memories, thing memories, memories of happenings — all these are valuable clues along the trails that led to our beginnings.

Surveys show that 90 percent of the people of the world either are grandparents or will be. Since that is true, it is not unreasonable to invite a bit of musing here: "What

PART III

kind of grandparent will I be?"

That is an important question for many reasons. Grandparents are for loving: for giving love; and for receiving love. But grandparents can also be a bridge from yesterday. So here are some things we think you might like to know about your grandfather and grandmother.

Your Grandfather

Birth date and place

Where he lived

Known facts about his growing up

Education

His first job

Employment

PART III

His toughest challenge

Religion, beliefs, values

Favorite sayings, quotations, Scripture

Special service or military service

Community work

Special interests

PART III

Your Grandmother

Birth date and place

Where she lived

Known facts about her growing up

Education

Her first job

Employment

Her toughest challenge

PART III

Religion, beliefs, values

Favorite sayings, quotations, Scripture

Special service or military service

Community work

Special interests

PART III

And some more of our favorite memories

How we met

Our engagement

Our wedding

Reception

Church

Maid (matron) of honor

Best man

Bridesmaids

Ushers

Other things we remember about that day

PART III

Our first years of marriage

Birth of our babies

Stories about us

PART III

Hobbies (sewing, gardening, music, fixing things, etc.)

Favorite foods, books, TV, radio, theater, sports, movies, hymns, poems, songs

The day your father (mother) was born

PART III

Some of our happiest memories

The hardest things we've gone through

Fun things we do now

PART III

Photographs

PART III

Photographs

PART IV

The Family Tree

PART IV

*"Look to the rock from which you were hewn;
the quarry from which you were digged."* **ISAIAH 51:1**

The Family Tree

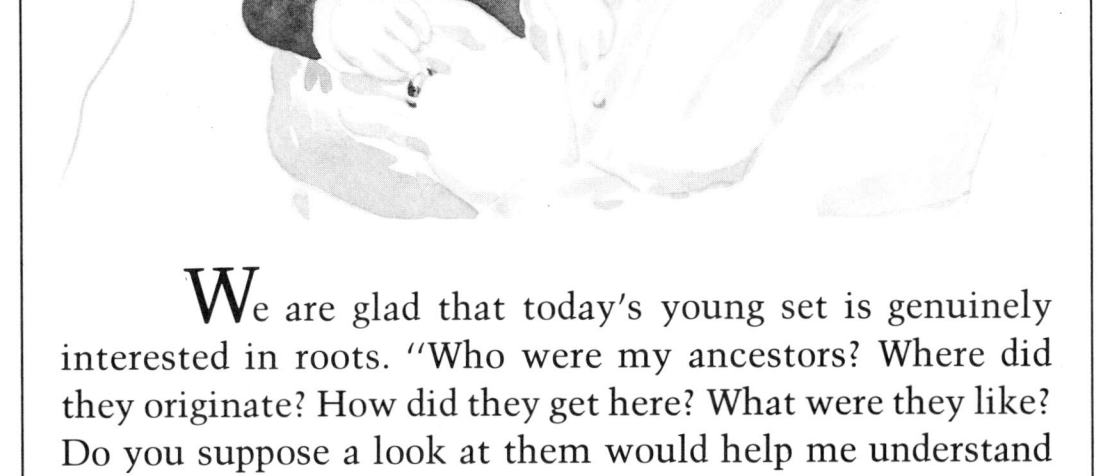

We are glad that today's young set is genuinely interested in roots. "Who were my ancestors? Where did they originate? How did they get here? What were they like? Do you suppose a look at them would help me understand me?"

Yes, and it could even open up a whole new world, as it did for these two:

They were a young married couple, and they thought antiques were strictly for strange characters, the nonprogressives. Then, one day, they came on an ancient table in her parents' basement. Scarred and blackened, this was one desolate item. But closer investigation turned up a fascinating history. This same musty table had been bought by her father and mother when they married, in 1912. Secondhand then, it had cost the struggling pair two dollars.

Suddenly, a new sentiment: a touch of respect for antiquity. Could something be done with this old piece? It could. Rescuing the table from its gloomy corner, they stripped it down to bare wood, and marveled. Rich golden oak, a magnificent memento of their own heritage. So here they are today, real antique buffs, rescuers of ancient beauties.

From old table in the basement to the history of personal characteristics, the new interest in things past is a real plus on today's scene. Backgrounds, bloodlines, pedigrees can be more than entertainment. Approached with reverence they may revive good things long gone. Is this one more reason the Good Book says, "Look to the rock from which you were hewn; the quarry from which you were digged."

Where various groups of the family came from

PART IV

*Where various groups of the family settled,
and how they got here*

Things we've heard about other ancestors

PART IV

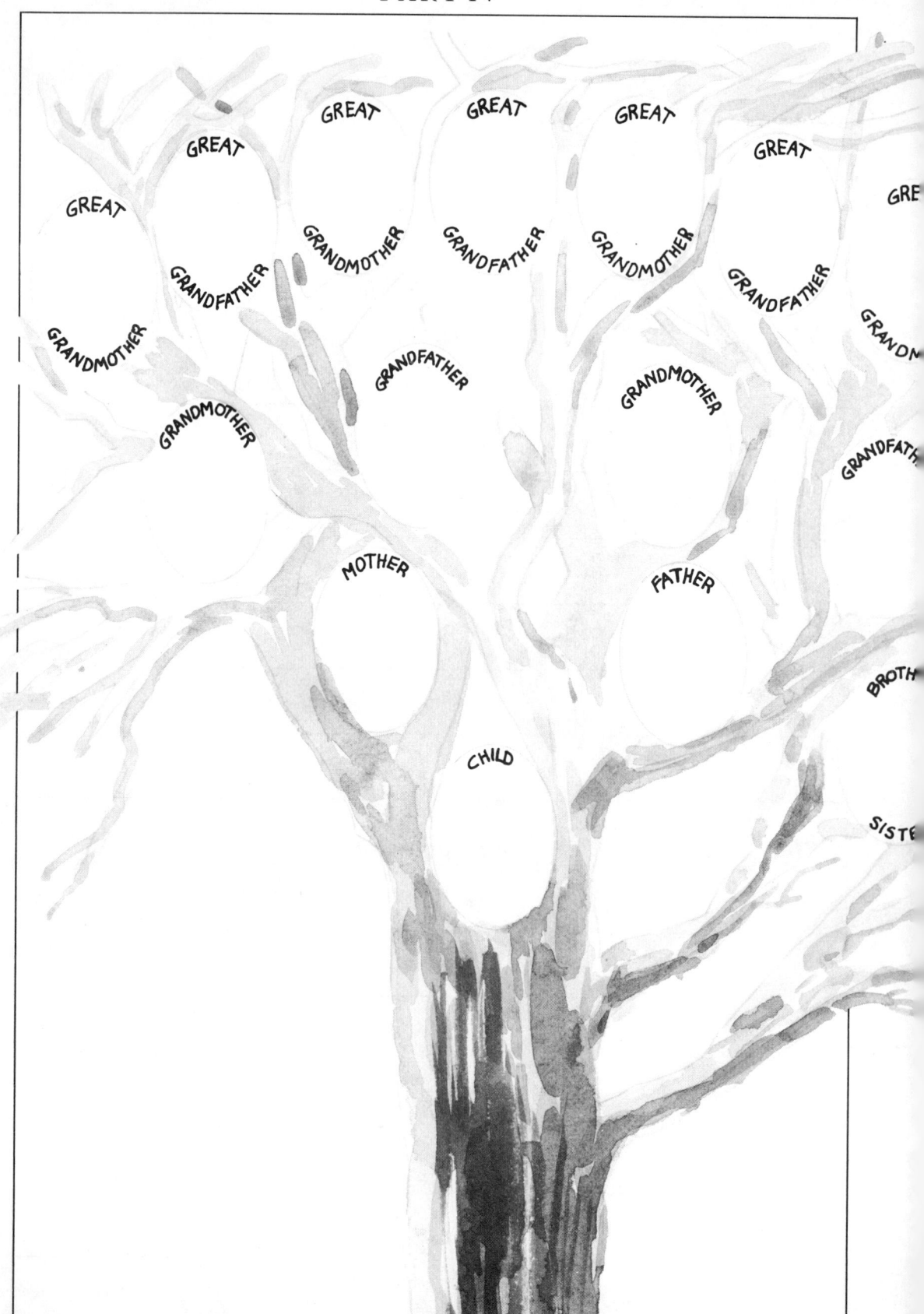

PART IV

GREAT
GRANDFATHER BROTHER
SISTER
SISTER
BROTHER

"...like a tree planted by the river, bringing forth fruit in season." **PSALM 1:3**

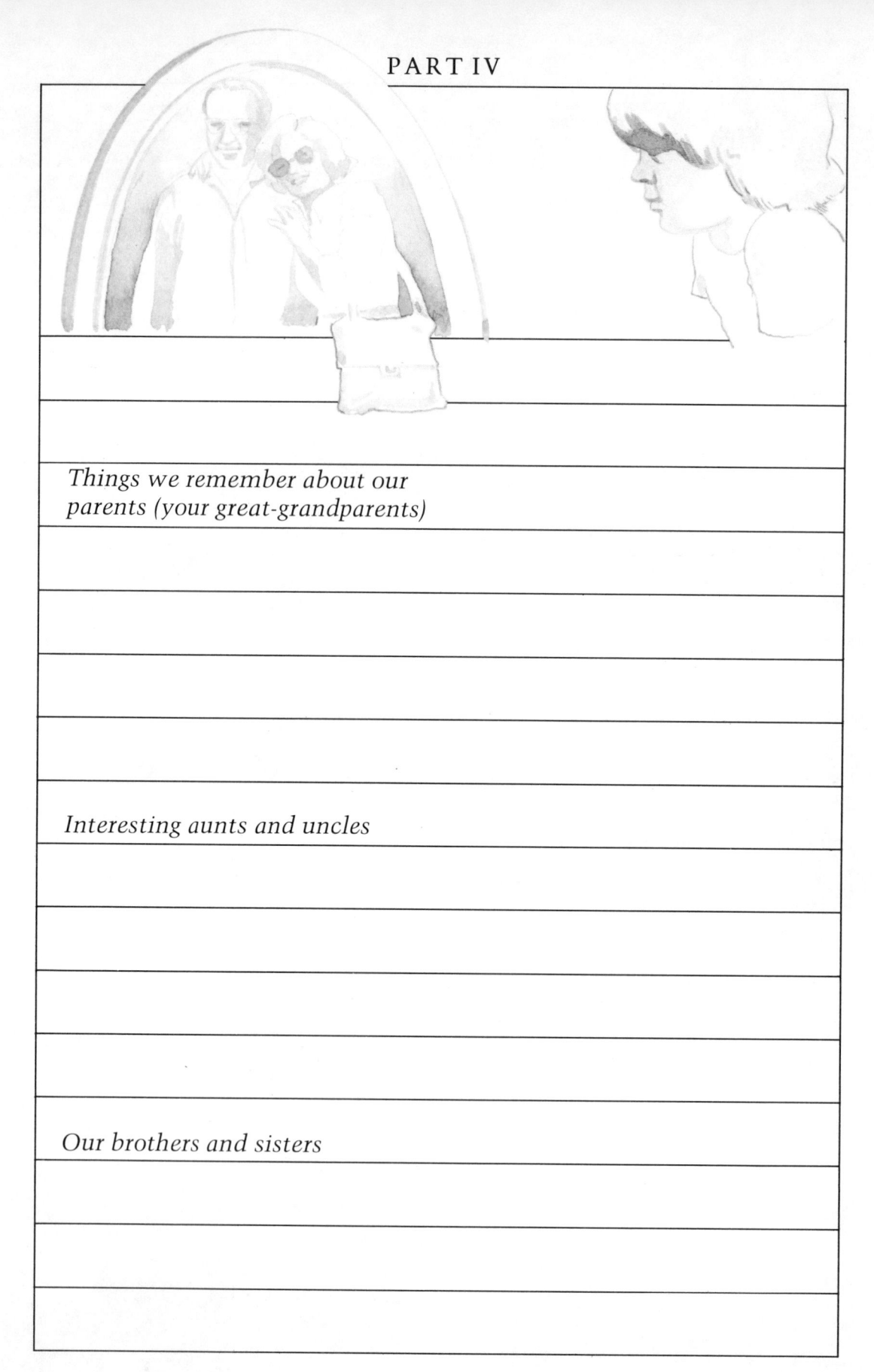

PART IV

Things we remember about our parents (your great-grandparents)

Interesting aunts and uncles

Our brothers and sisters

PART IV

Special stories about cousins

Special achievements

PART IV

*Family traits that
might be of special interest*

*Participation in historical events,
notable eras, politics, etc.*

PART IV

Photographs

PART V

General Family Attitudes

PART V

*"May the Lord, the God of our ancestors,
make you increase a thousand times more."* **DEUTERONOMY 1:11**

General Family Attitudes

They were sitting around in the neighborhood grocery store, cronies all. The discussion this day turned to college sons and daughters. A natural theme just then, because the next week was the start of Christmas vacation.

George was the center of attention at the moment. His eldest son had been ordained to the ministry the previous Sunday. He and his new wife would be going as missionaries to Haiti. Then they talked about George's daughter. She was at the top of her class in nursing school. They all knew that, because they'd seen it in the weekly paper. And now it was Wiley, George's youngest. Fast, big Wiley had made linebacker on the conference champions, and that was some deal for a university freshman.

From one of the chief jokers: "George, how come, with all these great kids, you never made the headlines?"

To which George smiled his craggy smile and came back with his usual something-to-think-about answer: "I'll tell you what: Ever since they were born, their mother and I have prayed that our kids would be an improvement on us."

Most parents, grandparents too, carry in their hearts this secret prayer: "May the God of our ancestors make you better than we were, a thousand times better."

Religion
Bringing up children/ family life
Philosophy of work
Success

PART V

Family habits

Money

Physical health

Mental health

PART V

*Thoughts on how your
tendencies may have originated*

*Thoughts on government, politics, world affairs,
whom the family voted for*

PART VI

Things We Did Together

PART VI

Things We Did Together

"Grandparents are for having fun with." This is the tribute of a junior-high grandson at the time of his grandmother's funeral.

"My grandmother was my very best friend. I mean my best friend ever. The winter before she died, she came to live where we did. Only, she had an apartment on the corner. Every night I'd get off the school bus and stop to see her. She would always be waiting for me by the window. Then we ate some cookies, had hot chocolate, lemonade, played games. We played 'kings and queens' and sometimes animals. She could meow exactly like a cat, and bark almost

PART VI

like a dog. We also played movie stars and people from our favorite TV programs. I could talk about everything around my grandma and imagine anything. She wouldn't laugh at me. Grandparents are the most fun, because they aren't afraid to pretend."*

What we thought when we heard you would be our next grandchild

The first time we saw you

The first time you visited us

Some of our favorite funnies about you

*Quoted from Charlie Shedd, *Then God Created Grandparents and It Was Very Good* (Garden City, N.Y.: Doubleday & Company, Inc. 1976).

PART VI

Things you said to us about:
"What I'd like to be when I grow up."

Some of your fantasies

Your imaginary playmates

PART VI

Times when we were especially proud

Times you were especially kind or thoughtful

PART VI

Times when you were naughty

Games we played

Work we did together

PART VI

Trips together

Other fun things we did with you

PART VI

Photographs

PART VII

Major Events of Your World and Some Before That

PART VII

"Days should speak, and multitude of years should teach wisdom." **JOB 32:7**

Major Events of Your World and Some Before That

Thought for pondering: Every forward leap of mankind—all the great discoveries; plus the tragedies, wars, economic depressions, freaks of nature—all these happenings in the years of men are not as important as what men do with them. And the same goes for women, and women and men together.

So, as your grandpa and grandma, we hope you remind yourself often:

*It isn't so much what happens to me;
It's what I do with what happens,
That makes the difference.*

95

PART VII

We also want you to sense this book is actually a kind of journey to some high hill for a panoramic view of one family, our heritage. But understanding the whole world is important too. The record of what has taken place in anyone's lifetime can provide some handles to the future.

Exciting discoveries during your lifetime and ours

New inventions

Space exploration

PART VII

New kinds of travels

*Medical discoveries,
big breakthroughs in research*

PART VII

Society, culture

Youth scene

PART VII

Environmental problems and challenges

Economy

PART VII

Leadership: local, national, international

Phenomena of nature: earthquakes, hurricanes, volcanoes, especially where members of the family may have been involved

PART VII

*"Days should speak,
and multitude
of years should teach wisdom."* **JOB 32:7**

Musings on the world of tomorrow.

PART VII

Newspaper Headlines
People and Places of the World

PART VII

Photographs

PART VIII

PART VIII

Special Days, Special Times

PART VIII

Special Days, Special Times

Why are some of the young so stable and others come apart in their teen years?

From a carefully conducted survey, here is one answer: Almost without variance the stable young look back to their home and family with warm recall. Anyone knows there are exceptions to every rule. Some behavior seems to defy explanation. Yet this was the finding. In the minds of those young who kept coming on strong, there were very likely to be positive memories of family togetherness, sharing, laughter, fun. And this is another interesting fact: Many of those positive memories centered on holidays, special events, celebrations, family traditions.

PART VIII

Halloween

Thanksgiving

PART VIII

Christmas traditions

Special Christmas celebrations

PART VIII

New Year's

Easter

Memorial Day

PART VIII

Fourth of July

Labor Day

Birthdays

PART VIII

Anniversaries

Sports, dancing class, music lessons

Family reunions

PART VIII

Vacations

Fun trips

Camp

PART VIII

Photographs

PART VIII

Photographs

PART IX

Other Little Things We Thought You'd Like to Know

PART IX

"...whatsoever things are lovely ...think on these things." **PHILIPPIANS 4:8**

Other Little Things We Thought You'd Like to Know

A visitor from France was asked by her American host, "If you could take back something from our country, what would it be?" Without a moment's hesitation, the visitor replied, "I would like one of those garbage cans where you step on the lever and the lid flies up."

Our lives are so much like that. We go from big event to big event, but in recall, the special times are often small mementos of our daily living.

"That rainy day on vacation when we saw all those rainbows."

"When a wren built her nest in our fern."

"That Sunday the dog came to church and found us in our pew."

PART IX

"A dream that came true."

"Painted buntings every spring at our bird feeder."

"The smell of a bonfire."

Is there any greater evidence of our Creator's wisdom than this? He made us with a special appreciation for life's little extras.

"...whatsoever things are lovely, think on these things." **PHILIPPIANS 4:8**

"I almost forgot to tell you"

Helpful ideas

PART IX

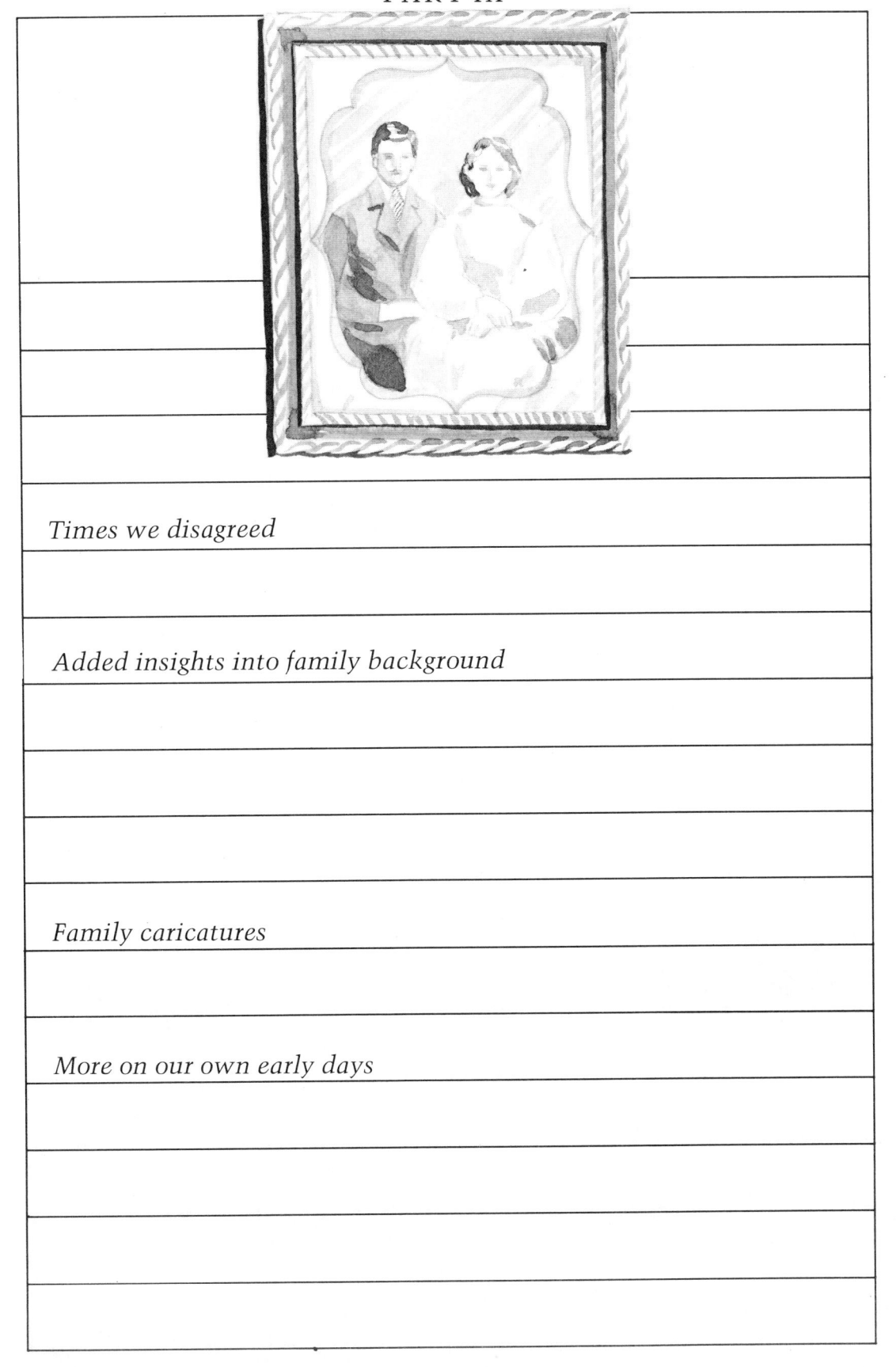

Times we disagreed

Added insights into family background

Family caricatures

More on our own early days

PART IX

Word of wisdom from grandparent to grandchild

My hopes for you

PART IX

Closing good wishes

PART IX

"...whatsoever things are lovely, think on these things." **PHILIPPIANS 4:8**

Final expression of love

PART IX

Photographs

Someday

The lord of a great estate was showing his special guest over the grounds. Amazing arrangements of bushes and flowers, carefully tended specimens—all of them together made the trip something to remember.

When they came to one small tree that seemed to be set apart, the guest inquired, "Why this unusual treatment?"

"Oh," answered the lord of the estate, "that tree blooms very rarely, but they say its flower is one of the most thrilling sights mankind could ever behold."

"You haven't seen it?" the guest asked. "Oh, no," came the answer. "My great-grandparents planted it. My grandparents nourished it carefully. My parents, too. And now I water and tend it. Someday someone of our family in generations to come will see it bloom."

Isn't that the hope of every family?

CHARLIE and MARTHA SHEDD have been married for more than forty years and are the happy grandparents of four grandchildren. In addition to Charlie's very active writing career (he is the author of several best-selling books including *Grandparents, Letters to Karen, Letters to Philip, The Stork is Dead* and *Talk to Me*), they both send their message of God's love and family enjoyment to others through their Marriage Enrichment seminars, a nationally syndicated television program, a series of five movies entitled "The Fun in Marriage Workshop," and are particularly active in the Abundance Foundation, which they set up and support, that provides grants for hunger relief around the world specifically through Christian agricultural missionaries.